From Tragedy to Triumph

Cindy's Story

Cindy Rogers

Copyright

Title: From Tragedy to Triumph: Cindy's Story

Author: Cindy Rogers

Publisher: Cindy Rogers

References:

Holy Bible, New King James Version. Unless otherwise noted all scripture is taken from The New King James Version: New Testament, 1979. Arthur Farstad et al., The New King James Bible, New Testament. Nashville: Thomas Nelson, 1979.

Holy Bible, 1982. Arthur Farstad, ed., Holy Bible: The New King James Version: Containing the Old and New Testaments. Nashville: Thomas Nelson, 1982.

Holy Bible, New Living Translation. p.33 Scripture quotations are taken from the Holy Bible, New Living Translation, copyright © 1996, 2004, 2015 by Tyndale House Foundation. Used by permission of Tyndale House Publishers, Inc., Carol Stream, Illinois 60188. All rights reserved

ISBN# 9798646403132

Acknowledgements

First, I want to thank my Lord and Savior, Jesus Christ, who brought me through the most difficult grieving process I have ever endured in my life. Without Jesus, I would have had no peace, no joy and no hope. Lord, you are faithful!

Thank you to my pastors who were there for me with encouraging words, loving kindness and several home visits, along with gifts and cards.

Thank you to my church family who expressed their concern and care for my son and me in so many ways. I appreciated their visits and phone calls.

Thank you to my friends and family, also neighbors who showed compassion to my son and me by making us meals, desserts, sending cards, flowers, visits and phone calls.

Thanks to the grocery store where my son worked at the time that gave us five to six brown paper bags of a variety of foods filled to the top. We had so much food in our home, actually we were running out of refrigerator and freezer space. I had to share it with others.

Thank you to my husband's best friend, Sam, who was with Roy when he took his last breath. Sam, you are a loyal friend to me and were to Roy, as well. My gratitude for you is deep and sincere.

I want to thank my son, Bryan, for helping me to be strong at the viewing and funeral. When I cried, you hugged me. You were concerned for your mom because you said I was lonely. Sometimes, you even stayed at home with me to have dinner together and to play a game instead of going out with your friends. I really appreciated that more than you ever knew.

Thank you to my brother, Tommy and my sister-n-law, Barbara for encouraging me to buy a dog, which they said, will help me not to be lonely. They made a special trip from Pennsylvania to New Jersey to take me to the pet store to buy a dog. I did. He became my friend.

I thank my second husband, Steve, for his encouragement and support that he gives me to write this book, along with editing it for me. He is hoping this book will help others who are going through the grieving process to hear my story of how the Lord brought me through it all.

I want to thank Kelly for her expertise in helping me publish this book. What a true blessing she has been.

Introduction

Doesn't our life's journey seem to be filled with ups and downs? You do not know what is up ahead or around the corner until it is in front of you. I had a picture over my sofa for years with beautiful flowers on it and a stone walkway that made a bend to the right, and you could not see where it went. I used to look at that picture and had even told a friend of mine, "that is what our lives are like." No one knows what each day will bring. The bend in the road is a mystery.

For some of us, our lives seem to go along more easily than others. I am not sure why that is, or maybe it just looks as though it is. We all have issues to face about which others do not even know. When issues do arise in our lives, stop and pray bringing them before the Lord. He is a loving God and waits for us to call upon His name. He wants to help us, and when we cry out to Him, He hears us. Truly believe in your heart with great expectations that He will.

I do not know what is around your bend that you could not see until it was in front of you, but for me, my husband of twenty-three years died on a hunting trip at a hunting camp in the tundra of Canada. I asked the Lord "what do I do now," and I trusted Him that He would lead me through this difficult time in my life.

I hope my story will inspire you to trust God more, become dependent on him, and believe He is always with you no matter where the bend in your road takes you.

"Cast all your anxiety on Him because He cares for you."
1 Peter 5:7

"So do not fear, for I am with you; do not be dismayed, for I am your God. I will strengthen you and help you; I will uphold you with my righteous right hand." Isaiah 41:10

Table of Contents

High School Days

Becoming a freshman in high school was a whole new experience than being in middle school. Leaving the middle school, I was at the top of the spectrum being the older student since the middle school was sixth, seventh and eighth graders. Entering into high school was a little intimidating because seniors were in that school and they were the "big" kids. It was exciting but scary at the same time. I had to remember where my classes were as the high school was on a much larger scale, and finding my locker was not easy at first. Anyway, I finally learned how to navigate around and actually got to my classes before the bell rang. Progress was in the making for me!

Going to high school was a time to explore new things and make some new friends. I liked my friends from the middle school; however, they were not all in the same classes as me. The classes I really enjoyed were home economics class, sewing class, early childhood education classes not so much the math, history and science classes. Of course, I had to take all those classes as well. I chose all business courses, not college courses. I was never encouraged at home to attend college - only that I should get a job after attending high school. So, with that in mind, I had already decided that I would take business courses.

Kids in the tenth grade wanted to become friends with me and my friends, but we really liked being with people we knew. There was so much going on in high school - dances, events, pep rallies for the football games on Friday nights, etc. My friends and I had a great time together.

After school we would stop by the sweet shop for a vanilla coke and a hamburger. We played a lot of pinball, which I really enjoyed, and just talked with our friends before walking home. I decided I really liked high school - it was fun. The homework was not fun, but I kept up with it and received decent grades. As the freshman year ended, we had the school end dance, and everyone signed our yearbooks that night. People I did not know very well signed my yearbook - not sure why? Wow, the year went fast, and now I was going on to become a sophomore.

As my sophomore year began, the school was all familiar to me, I knew exactly where the lockers were, however, in a different hallway. Now, the freshmen were beginning their first year, and I knew how they felt because I was once in their place not long ago. I would help them to their classes or lockers if they seemed to be lost in the halls.

The year seemed to be going by quickly - dances were happening and pep rallies on Friday nights. We had so much fun at the pep rallies and wanted our football team to win the game the next day. We had a really great football team. Most of the boys on the team were built husky and looked strong. I guess they worked out hard in the gym to build up their muscles to be tough on the team. I understood there was a boy on the team that liked me. I really never noticed him, but he noticed me. He was a junior and I was a sophomore. His name was Roy. We were both sixteen years old. I found out later he liked me when I was a freshman age fifteen.

When I was fifteen and soon turning sixteen, I had a really big sweet sixteen party at a nice banquet hall. I invited maybe fifty or more kids to this party. At the time, there was another boy who liked me who was a junior in our school; I did invite him to the party along with Roy. The other boy was driving and Roy had made arrangements for him to pick him up at a meeting place in town. The boy who liked me just went to the party without picking up Roy and it was too far for him to walk to the party so Roy never came. I did however, go out with this boy a few times before going out with Roy.

Roy and I got to be friends and went out a few times. He came over to my house and we played cards and took walks in the park next to my house. When he got a car, we would go to the movies and out to eat. We also went to the beach and walked on the boardwalk. In February, 1969, he came over to my house and asked me how would I like to hold his ring (high school ring) for a while. I said yes and that meant we were going steady. I had a HIS pin where I would pin it to my shirt and attach his ring on it with a chain clip of some sort. I also wore his ring on a chain hanging around my neck. It was cool to have a boyfriend on the football team.

We continued to be boyfriend and girlfriend throughout the rest of high school.

Wedding Bells

Roy and I continued our relationship after high school for three more years before getting engaged. We were both twenty-one years old. After discussing which month in we wanted to be married, we agreed on a June wedding. It was the most popular month, springtime. I chose my maid of honor and bridesmaids and Roy chose his best man and his groomsmen. I had selected the colors of the bridesmaid's gowns and the groomsmen tuxes. We visited several venues to find the best deals. My brother's friend was a photographer, and my sister-n-law knew people in a band. Wow, things were moving along pretty quickly. My sister-n-law made my wedding gown and helped me with ordering flowers, favors and all the details for the wedding. I was very close with my sister-n-law since my parents were divorced when I was five; so, my mother was not a part of my wedding.

I was not close with my dad since he was an alcoholic and abusive. After my parents were divorced, he remarried years later to a woman who was addicted to prescription medications. Their marriage also ended in a divorce. During my childhood years, I grew up in a very dysfunctional home where there was no love or encouragement. My dad would say things to me like; "You are too stupid to attend college," and "I am not going to waste my money on you." He also would repeatedly tell me that I would never amount to anything - such hurtful words.

In addition to emotional abuse, he became violent when drinking. One night after returning home from a date with Roy, I came into the house and my dad started screaming at me that he was going to kill me. I ignored him and went to my bedroom which was in the basement where there was only one exit. He was in the kitchen, and I think he went over to the knife drawer… he was serious about what he said he was going to do. Before he could get to the basement steps, God made a way for me to escape. I ran to my next-door neighbor's house at midnight and, thankfully, they let me in. I was scared, and my heart was pounding. I called Roy immediately, and he picked me up at my neighbor's house. We went to his parent's house making them aware of what happened. I slept on their couch in the living room. Roy's family had accepted me into their family when we began dating at age sixteen and now at eighteen. I was very blessed because it was the family I never had.

After the incident took place with my dad, I moved out of my home since I did not have a choice, due to unsafe conditions. God provided me with a good job with the State of New Jersey. My brother co-signed on a studio apartment for me - a place I called home where I felt safe. After two years, God blessed me with a better paying job, and a large one - bedroom apartment, where Roy and I would reside after the wedding.

For quite a long time I did not have communication with my dad. He did not know where I was living, and I did not want him to know. My brother was out of the home and married but kept in touch with him. I heard through my brother that my dad was married for the third time.

My dad's third wife called me one day and somehow knew that I was getting married. I was not sure how she found my phone number; maybe my brother gave it to her. She said that my dad would like to walk me down the aisle, and he would like the wedding party to leave from his house. I was more than surprised that she was calling and not my dad. I told her I would think about it, and give her a call back.

After a few days of thinking about it, I called her back and said yes, I had decided he could walk me down the aisle, and the wedding party could leave from his home. He also said he would give me money toward the wedding. Our wedding was at 4:00 pm, and I told him he was not to drink during the day of the wedding, or I would never speak to him again. He respected what I had told him and did not drink before the ceremony. Even though I never got an apology from him for the mean things he said and did, for the terrible names he called me and for attempting to kill me, I chose to forgive him. He did walk me down the aisle, and the wedding party left from his home. Forgiveness is not always easy, but it is what the Lord commands us to do.

"Be kind and compassionate to one another, forgiving each other, just as in Christ God forgave you." Ephesians 4:32

Our wedding was beautiful, and the weather was perfect. My dad looked very happy at the church to be walking his daughter down the aisle on her "special" day. To think, he almost missed this special day, since things could have turned out differently, until I decided to forgive him.

Our Gift

For the first seven years of our married life, Roy and I enjoyed having fun on the weekends. We both worked full-time and looked forward to spending time with friends and family.

We decided it was time to start our family. My first pregnancy ended in a miscarriage. We were very upset, but I did become pregnant again. I had some difficulty with this pregnancy, also. I prayed to God, asking Him to please let me carry this baby to full term; I wanted to be a mommy. As the months went on, I had less issues and I truly believed in my heart that I was going to carry full term. I did. Praise the Lord! He gave us a baby boy, and we named him Bryan.

When Bryan was three years old, it was time to have a second child. The pregnancy was going well, but in the second trimester something terrible happened. My doctor's visit that month did not go well. She told me she could not hear the heartbeat, and the month before she did hear it. The doctor requested that I go to the hospital and have a sonogram done on a larger screen. Next day I went to the hospital and had the sonogram. The doctor came in afterward and had a sad look on her face. She told me the baby died, and made a comment that I had a hard time carrying girls. Both miscarriages were baby girls.

I know they are back in heaven with the Lord, but the pain was piercing. I left the hospital and cried all the way home. I did not know what happened to my baby girl and I surely did not want to believe she died. I found out the next day that I could not have the surgical procedure done for another week because that particular area of the hospital was full. I had to carry around this baby knowing she was dead for another week. To make matters worse, I worked at a day care center in the nursery department, so every day of the week before I had the procedure done, I took care of infants. It was a very sad time for me. I know God was with me giving me the strength to endure this pain. After I had the procedure done the following week, and came home from the hospital, my son, Bryan, cried and said "why did that hospital take my baby from me?" I cried and my family that was there, cried. My heart was full of grief, sorrow and sadness. It took me awhile to overcome the loss.

We were so happy that God gave us our son to love and nurture. He was a challenge at times being an only child. Bryan turned out to be a fine man, a great husband and a wonderful daddy to his children. I have three grandchildren, two boys and a girl. God did give me a girl, my granddaughter! He is so good!

Step of Faith

My husband and I had been renting apartments, townhomes and a couple of houses ever since we had been married. We decided it was time for us to buy our first home because Bryan needed to be established in a neighborhood with other children. This was a step of faith because we really did not have a large down payment which was almost always required. I had faith in God that He would open a door for us. At the time, we were renting a townhouse and the owner decided that he wanted to sell it.

We were happy in that community and wanted to buy it. My husband and I applied for a mortgage, but the loan did not get approved; our down payment was not enough. At this point, we were very disappointed, but we kept looking since we were determined not to give up. There had to be a house some where we could afford.

Determined to find a home we started looking in a different area closer to where my in-laws lived. Actually, my mother-n-law heard there was a home for sale in a beautiful area near her. My husband and I made an appointment to go see the house one evening, and my in-laws met us there.

The property was beautiful, and the outside of the house looked nice. It was on a cul-de-sac with two and a half acres of property. Both the front and back yards were big. Behind the house was eleven hundred acres of woods. It was a national game forest called Ken Lockwood Gorge. The good thing was that no one could build behind the house. The drive way was curvy and steep, one-hundred and eighty-five feet to the front porch; it was very private and quiet. The house needed a lot of work inside. Both my husband and myself are good with remodeling and decorating, so that would not be a problem. The owners had reduced the price of the house substantially because they were getting a divorce and needed the money for their daughter's college. They told us the asking price for the house and it was ok. We liked it and wanted to buy it. The problem was that this house cost more than the townhouse and our loan was denied then, so how would we be able to afford this home? A few days later my in-laws talked to their son, Roy, and said they would loan us the money for the down payment if we wanted this home. Wow! I was really surprised and, yes, we did take them up on their offer to help us out. We applied for the loan and it was accepted, so we were now home owners. Thank the Lord!

The day came, and we were very excited to be moving into a home of our own. My son, who was seven, soon to be eight, loved having a yard and a basement with a play room. He soon met some boys in the neighborhood, one in particular with who he is still friends to this day. He started a new school in January that year but seemed to adjust pretty easily. Before long he made more friends and was involved in sports. School and sports kept him busy. On Sundays we did attend church, we tried a couple in the area and decided on a small country church close to home.

I was so grateful to God that he provided us with a nice home in a good neighborhood in which to raise our son. Before we knew it, Bryan was in middle school, then on to high school.

For many years, we had good times in our home and made lots of memories together.

Week of Distance

It was summertime, August, 1999. The days were hot, and the pool felt refreshing. Roy and I would spend time in the pool and on the back deck in the evenings, just talking about different topics. He had planned a big hunting trip with his best friend Sam which was coming up soon, so he was excited to talk about the details of the trip. He said they would leave for Canada on Thursday August 26th to hunt for caribou. He was explaining to me about flying to Canada then getting on another plane to Kuujjuaq which means "Fort Chimo" in English. He went on to say that they are flown into a hunting camp which is far into the tundra of Canada. He told me he was going to shoot two caribou on this trip.

The week went on and as it grew closer to Thursday it seemed as though we really did not talk much. He would eat dinner and watch some TV and fall asleep. I thought he must be really tired from working in the summer heat this week. He was an air conditioning and heating foreman, and worked outside, also in hot attics installing air conditioning in homes. I felt this hunting trip would be good for him to get away from the pressure of work, the summer heat and to do something he really enjoyed. Roy was an advent hunter and fisherman. He loved both sports and looked forward to either being in the woods hunting or on his boat fishing.

It really was a quiet week between us. I wanted to spend time together on the deck talking in the evening, but it was apparent that he did not. I left him alone and kept busy doing other things.

The Last Kiss

It was Wednesday, August 25th, the night before Roy and Sam were to leave for their hunting trip in the morning. The evening was so nice outside, and Roy actually wanted to go out on the deck and talk. We sat on the deck and talked for a bit about our day. He then looked at me and said "Is the life insurance paid up?", (since I was the bookkeeper in the house). I said, "Yes, it's always paid up." He did not say anything for a few minutes: he just sat there. Then he said let's go down to the basement; that's where his workshop was. I said okay. We went down to the basement where the rack of his fishing poles and reels were hanging on the wall. He looked at me and said, "If I don't come back, give this fishing pole to Bryan, and this one with the big expensive reel on it goes to my cousin, and this one goes to my dad." There were other poles he said went to someone, but I stopped him and said "Are you trying to tell me something"? He replied, "You never know what can happen", I was a bit puzzled about this reply. Then we walked me over to his workshop. He opened up a metal cabinet on the wall and proceeded to show me and tell me "Here are the keys to the boat and the trailer" also, he showed me where the ammunition was for the guns that were locked up in the gun safe. I really was not feeling at peace with all this information he was giving me. It sounded like he was not coming back. We went upstairs, he went to take a shower then off to bed, since he had to get up early in the morning to leave at 5:00 am. I was upset about our conversation. I felt like he was trying to tell me something, without telling me something… hmmm.

The morning came for him to leave on the hunting trip. We were both up early, since I wanted to say goodbye to him. He seemed to be in a big hurry. Before heading for the door to leave, he gave me a kiss but a quick peck, and I said, "Wait, I want another kiss - that was too quick." I could tell he was getting anxious to leave but he did stop, gave me another kiss and said goodbye. I walked him to the door and closed it behind him.

Tragedy Strikes

This chapter is Sam's best recollection of the events that happened on the hunting trip as told to me over 20 years later.

Roy left with Sam on Thursday, August 26,1999, at 5:00 am to beat the traffic. They were stopping at his sister's house on Lake Champlain, New Hampshire to pick up a very large cooler to take with them to Canada. The need for this cooler was to store the anticipated caribou meat for the trip back home. After that, Roy and Sam drove to Montreal, Canada; they went to a hotel by the airport. Roy parked his fairly new pickup truck in the hotel parking lot in a special long-term lot for the hunting group. When he parked his truck, he told Sam he was going to disable the truck to prevent theft by taking the ignition fuse from the fuse box and the wire connector from the distributor. He told Sam, "If anything happens to me, this is where I put them" and Sam replied "Nothing is going to happen." Sam did not pay attention to where Roy hid the car parts.

They stayed at the hotel one night, then left for Kuujjuaq on Friday morning. The flight from Montreal was about two hours to Kuujjuaq. From there, they were flown into the camp on a small plane. When they arrived, it was a beautiful sunny day; however, the weather changes abruptly up there. The guide took them by motor boat across Snow Goose Lake and dropped Roy and Sam off in the hilly green barren grounds of northern Quebec. Roy and Sam separated and took to the hills. Once they got into the hills it looked like rain was coming, and it did start raining. They had rain ponchos in their packs. The storm was really bad, rain, lightening, thunder sleet, hail and 50mph winds. The temperature dropped to 30 degrees. The storm lasted about thirty minutes; then it all calmed down. They both saw caribou and decided to wait for it. Roy got his first caribou around 4:00 pm on his first day, Friday, August 27, 1999. The guide helped them load the caribou into a boat and take it back to the camp and shared stories with other hunters.

At this point, they learned the storm took out the antenna for the satellite radio, and they had no contact with the home base in Kuujjuaq - no way to communicate with the outside world at all.

The night came and the guys were back in their cabins. Sam said Roy was snoring very loudly - extremely loud. It was unbearably loud with possible stopping like sleep apnea. He seemed to get through the night, but Sam asked him if he was okay because of his breathing last night. I am not sure of his reply.

They went out the next day on Saturday looking for caribou but did not see anything. Sam said Roy was getting edgy due to frustration and anxiety about getting a big caribou. Although he got one on the first day of the hunt, he was worried that they were not seeing any more caribou, and he wanted to get another one. He became more edgy and cantankerous.

On Sunday, August 29th they went out again together. They saw caribou and Roy stalked a big one and asked Sam to stay behind so he could be quiet and crawl up to the critter and shoot it. Sam heard him shoot and went over to congratulate Roy. They were taking pictures and Roy said to Sam "you have got to get my picture" and Sam took several of them. At that point they were standing next to each other (back to back) and Sam heard a thud and turned and saw Roy was on the ground and there was no life in him. Sam checked his pulse, made sure his air way was clear, started CPR the best he could do, tapped his face, his eyes were rolled back.

Sam started shooting SOS's 3 shots pause then one shot (he did this 3 times) to get the guide. Sam did not leave Roy alone and stayed with him until the guide went to get help. Six guys (some of the other hunters) carried his body down to the boat and from the boat back to the camp.

The plane had just come, and someone fixed the antenna. They then were able to contact the home base to tell them what happened. They sent a plane in to pick up Sam and Roy, and took them back to Kuujjuaq. The plane was met by an ambulance and took Roy's body to the hospital, and Sam went with the hunters in the group to the hospital. Sam waited in the hospital over night while they examined Roy to determine the cause of death. Roy died from cardiac arrhythmia, which is a problem with the rate or rhythm of the heartbeat. He died immediately.

On Sunday, August 29th, 1999, he died, and his body was not flown back to Montreal from Kuujjuaq until the following Tuesday. Sam saw men load the casket onto the plane. From Montreal his body was to be flown to Newark, New Jersey, and the funeral home would pick up his body.

Shock

At 12:45a.m. on Monday morning, August 30th, my in-law's along with my sister-in-law's boyfriend came to my house and told me something happened to Roy. Without knowing the story, I just blurted out "He died." It just came right out. "Yes, he died", my mother-n-law said. Everyone was crying, and my son ran down the hall to his bedroom and slammed the door. I don't think it hit me yet because I did not see his body. He was in Canada on a hunting trip and died, how could that be?

It was almost like he knew somehow that he was not coming back from this hunting trip alive. The night before he left his asking me if the life insurance was paid up, and showing me the fishing poles and reels in the basement and saying who they should go to if he does not come back, along with where the boat and trailer keys were; it was all to beginning to make sense now. Also, wanting his friend Sam to know where the parts were hidden in his pick-up truck in case anything happened to him and he would have to drive the truck back to New Jersey. Did he

know, or how did he know he was not returning. I began
to cry and went in the other room. I felt alone, so sad, I
missed him already. I did not want to believe he was dead.
I did not even know where his body was at this point. It
all felt like a bad dream, but it was not a dream; this was
real.

My heart actually ached and I could feel myself
trembling. The loss of someone you have been with from
the age of sixteen years old was beyond words. Roy was
only forty-five years old. In my mind, he was too young to
die. He had a wife and a sixteen-year son to be here for.
But all that did not matter because he was gone. Nothing
we could do would bring him back to his family. We
would now go through grief, we would mourn, live in pain
and sorrow, but I knew this and believed this, that God
was going through it with us!

Jesus said in Matthew 5:4 *"Blessed are those who mourn, for
they will be comforted."*

Dreadful Arrangements

In a few days, Roy's body would be coming back to New Jersey, and the planning of the funeral was underway. So many thoughts were going through my mind about the funeral. First, I have to meet with the funeral director to discuss when the viewing would take place, selecting a casket, meet with my pastors who will be officiating the funeral, going to the florist to select flowers and so on - floods of thoughts flashing through my mind. I was not ready to bury my husband, but knew I had to do this.

I contacted the funeral home to see when I would be able to come. The funeral home in our small town was owned by a friend of mine from church. He was very nice, kind and caring to me. We set up a time to meet at the funeral home on Tuesday, August 31st. I called my in-laws to see if they would like to meet me there and they said yes, also my husband's sister met us there, as well. My son, Bryan, did not want to be there and that was fine with me. He was dealing with the death of his dad in his own way.

Tuesday came, and we all met out front of the funeral home. When I walked in, I felt my heart racing and was very uneasy. I still did not want to believe I was planning my husband's funeral, but this was reality. We all settled into the funeral director's office and sat quietly for a few minutes, staring at one another. The meeting then began and the director asked me what time I wanted the viewings, day and evening, and what time the funeral would be. I said I wanted a viewing only one day, two times, one early afternoon and early evening. I requested the funeral to be in the morning. Roy's parents agreed and really did not say much - probably just letting me make the arrangements for everything.

I then had to go through several pictures choosing the casket in which he would be laid. I picked one out that his parents liked as well. This was so difficult to do, and it must have broken his parents heart having to bury their son so young. We, of course, discussed the fees for the funeral and all the extra charges that were involved. We talked about flowers at the funeral home and gravesite. Our meeting was over, and we all left together. What a sad moment for all of us.

My mother-in-law and sister-in-law and I decided to go to the florist and order the flowers for the casket and the grave. All this was happening so fast, but the viewings were in two days and the funeral in three days. I also had to meet with the pastors to arrange the funeral service so they would have time to print the itinerary of the service. The funeral was on Labor Day weekend, September 4th, so I had to give the church enough time to prepare, in case people were going away.

After we went to the florist, I was really exhausted and my heart was hurting. I had not slept much since the news of his death. My sorrow was so deep, I literally was walking around in a daze. I do believe this was God's way of protecting me from the grief and despair I was experiencing.

I went home and cried a lot; I needed a double dose of God's comfort. He heard my cries, and I could feel His peace cover me. I think I fell asleep…in His loving arms.

"You keep track of my sorrows. You have collected all my tears in your bottle. You have recorded each one in your book." Psalm 56:8 (NLT)

I had cried so many tears, I am sure my bottle overflowed, but the Lord has collected them all.

Final Moments

Roy's body was flown back from Montreal, Canada on Wednesday, September 2nd to Newark, New Jersey, and where the funeral home had made the arrangements to pick him up. He arrived at the funeral home later that day. I had to bring the clothes to the funeral home in which Roy was going to buried. Knowing he did not like to be dressed in a suit, I buried him in his favorite clothes - jeans and a flannel shirt.

The next day, the viewing was in the early afternoon and again in the evening. My son and I went to the funeral home an hour before the time others would be coming. I walked over to the casket and had tears running down my face. I tried to compose myself, but I could not stop crying. My son and I stood there looking at Roy for a few minutes. He looked like the Roy I knew for all those years, but just sleeping. I walked away from the casket and went into the other room with my son. He saw me crying and he hugged me. At that time, my in-laws were coming into the funeral home. They all walked over to the casket and stared at Roy. All I could hear was crying, and we hugged each other. There were no words anyone could say that would help what we were all experiencing at that moment. Losing one person we all loved had an effect on all of us. My in-laws lost their son, my sister-n-law lost her brother, my son lost his dad, I lost my husband and my sister-n-law's boyfriend lost a good friend. All of us were grieving and feeling pain.

The hour had passed for the family to be there first and then people started to come. Every person came over to the family and said how sorry they were for us. I could hear people talking, but I was in a groggy state of mind, so it sounded like a bunch of chatter.

At one point, I saw my son walk over to his dad's casket. He just stood there looking at him. I watched my in-laws standing at the casket, staring at their son. Also, his sister and her boyfriend standing at the casket, all with sadness in their hearts.

Visiting hours for the afternoon viewing were coming to a close until the evening viewing. We stayed until everyone was gone. The funeral director helped us to the door and said he would see us that evening.

Just like earlier, my son and I and my in-laws came early to the evening viewing before the others started coming in. There were a lot of people, friends, family, acquaintances, neighbors, bosses, co-workers and so on. Roy used to tell me he did not have many friends; there were hundreds of people just pouring in to pay their respects to the family.

At the afternoon viewing, a small company that I used to work for years ago actually closed the office so the people that I worked with could attend the viewing. The love and caring hearts in that room was just beyond words.

I walked over to the casket and looked at him. Grief-stricken, heartbroken and just so sad, I cried. While I was standing there, I noticed some pictures in the casket, pictures of Bryan and his dad, and I picked up the pictures to look at them. I accidentally dropped the pictures on the floor and they landed face down. I saw writing on the back. Bryan had written heart-felt messages to his dad on the back of those pictures. The one I read said "Dad, I am so proud of the accomplishments you have made in your life", and I began to cry; I could not continue to read it anymore, since I felt so sorry for Bryan to be without his dad. Such final moments sprinkled with true emotions of love from his son.

The viewing was over for the evening and the people began to leave. I wanted to be the last person out, spending a little time alone with Roy, since the casket would be closed tomorrow at the funeral, so I would not see him again. I stood by the casket for a few minutes and talked to Roy, I told him some things, even though he could not hear me. I touched his arm and told him I loved him and will miss him. The funeral director came in and said he had to close the casket.

I left the room and exited the building. Only by the grace of God was I able to get through my husband's two viewings. I needed more of the Lord's grace and His strength to get through tomorrow at the funeral and cemetery.

Ending of a Beginning

I hardly slept that night after the viewings. My emotions were all twisted up in a ball thinking about the funeral tomorrow. I guess I fell asleep at some point in the night. The funeral was at 10:00am. I was informed by the ladies at the church that we were having a big luncheon after the cemetery services. Everyone would come back to the church banquet hall to celebrate Roy's life and fellowship with one another.

My son and I were ready to go to the church. I was doing okay until we arrived at the church; then I became a little nervous. When I walked in and saw Roy's casket at the front of the church near the kneeling rail, I took a deep breath and walked forward down the aisle. We sat in the front of the church but on the right side of the aisle. Many people started to come into the church and look our way. The pastor started the funeral, prayed, read Scripture and sang a couple of songs. The service was over, and the pallbearer's carried the casket outside and put it in the hearse. We were on our way to the cemetery which was not far from the church. It was up a hill next to a church that played carillon's in the afternoon. The plot that was chosen for Roy was the last one backing up to the woods. He liked hunting in the woods, so I thought that would be a good place for him. At his grave I went up to the casket and placed a rose on it, then I stepped back, with tears in my eyes and sorrow in my heart. Later that day the cemetery custodians would lower the casket with my husband into the ground.

Roy was my boyfriend at sixteen, my fiancé at twenty-one, and my husband, age twenty-two for twenty-three years. Our wedding vows, till death do us part were lived out. This was the ending of our beginning.

After the service at the cemetery, many people came back to the church for the luncheon. We were going to eat and fellowship, and celebrate the life of Roy Taylor with friends and family. I so appreciated the ladies at the church who put on this luncheon; there was so much food and many desserts. People stayed for a least an hour or more talking with the family, telling stories of good times they had with Roy on fishing trips, and how he was a good friend to many people. They said he will be missed. The funeral was over. The luncheon was over. It was time for us to go home. My son and I went home together. His friends wanted him to go out with them that night, but he was not sure if he should, since he did not want to leave me alone. I encouraged him to go with his friends; I assured him I would be fine. He decided to go.

God's Comfort

As my son and his friends left the house, I stood at the front door watching them drive off. I closed the door and there I was alone, sad, and tearful. The house seemed so quiet, almost awkward. During the past week, there were so many people in the house - family, friends, my son's friends, neighbors and pastors. I began to feel a little uneasy and even anxious like I did not want to be in the house alone. Then I realized I was not alone; God was with me. I talked to Him and cried. My heart was broken, shattered and crushed. God's peace would come over me, and the crying would cease for a while. The tears came in waves, bursts of tears would flow from my eyes like a water fountain that would not shut off. I was so overwhelmed. Everything happened so fast from August 29,1999, the day Roy died, until September 4th, 1999, the day he was buried.

Crying is part of grieving, and it's healthy. If I did not cry and let my emotions out, they would have built up inside, and one day I would have had a breakdown. In the

Bible John 11:35 says *"Jesus wept."* He wept out of
sympathy with those in tears around Him. Jesus
compassionately understood my tears.

Later that evening my son returned home. Bryan
needed to be with his friends, and I needed to be home
alone with God. My son did not say much about the
funeral. I could tell his heart ached, and I sensed his
sadness. I was so sorry for him, putting my own sadness
aside. When our children hurt, we as parents hurt more. I
asked him how he was doing, "He said I am okay," and
went to his bedroom.

I could not sleep. I laid there thinking about what took
place the past two days. I cried so much that day and night
that my eyes inside actually hurt. The Lord was the only
one who could feel my pain. I told God, "I missed Roy so
much," and "tell him I loved him."

The next day, my friends called to see how I was doing.
They felt so bad, and I could hear the sadness in their
hearts that Roy was gone. My friends and neighbors
would ask me, "How are you dealing with this?" I would
say, "My faith is strong in God."

A few days following the funeral, Bryan returned to
school. That first week after the funeral I was going to
focus on getting the house in order, do the laundry, and
unpack Roy's belongings which were returned to me from
the hunting trip. As I started to take the clothes out of the
bag, the tears started flowing more and more. I was in the
first phase of grief – denial. I said to myself, "I am going

to hang up the hunting jackets and pants just how he would like them," thinking he was going to return. Denial - I knew he had died and was buried, but my mind wasn't ready to accept his death.

The next day, I went outside on the deck and started talking to the Lord. I told him "I feel so sad, and I need to know you are here with me." We had a windchime on the deck. It was not a windy day, rather very still out. The windchime started to tingle and move, ever so softly. I knew that it was the Lord. He was letting me know He was right there with me. God was comforting me with His presence.

Roy's birthday was on Sept 24th, 3 weeks after he was buried. My brother, Tommy, and his wife, Barbara, who lived in Pennsylvania called me and said I should have a dog. I was not sure about a dog. I loved dogs, but maybe it was not the right time. He went on to say a schnauzer would be a good dog for me, because they are small and very good watch dogs. He said a dog will keep me company, especially because Bryan will be out doing things with friends, at football practice, karate etc. I had a full-time job, a house, a son to drive back and forth to his activities, church choir rehearsals, and other responsibilities at the church. I was still not sure if I wanted a dog. Anyway, my brother and his wife came to my house on Saturday. We went to one pet store; that's it. In a cage was a schnauzer five and a half months old. I saw him, but I was not sure he was the one. My sister-n-law, Barbara, said "let's take him out of the cage." He was small and very cute. He crawled up on my lap and instantly he liked me, and I liked him. Barbara said to the clerk jokingly, "Wrap him up, she will take him."

I think God wanted me to have this dog because as we were walking into the store I said outside to my brother, "I have a name picked out, Toby." Yes, I bought Toby, a crate, food, toys, collar and a leash. Wow… everything took place so fast. God is good all the time! My brother and sister-n-law were right. Toby kept me company, and I did not feel alone in the house anymore.

I returned back to my full-time job three weeks after my husband died. The office where I worked was close by, so every day I would come home for lunch, take Toby out and play with him. I was very happy to have gotten him, and he was glad to have found his forever home. I found out the pet store was closing soon. He was a full pedigree and had papers, but the pet store closed, and I never received them. If I had not bought him, I am not sure what would have happened to him.

God comforts us in ways we do not even know. We went for walks in the park almost every day. Toby enjoyed car rides and hiking in the woods and just being with me. We were friends. God knew I needed Toby, and God knew Toby needed me!

"And we know that all things work together for good to those who love God, to those who are the called according to His purpose." Romans 8:28

Moving On

It was time to make plans to sell the house and decide
where I was going to live. My son, Bryan, would be going
off to college after graduation. I was at a fork in the road
of either staying in New Jersey and buying a home at the
beach area, or moving to Florida. As time went on, I
could feel in my spirit I should move to Florida. I prayed
and felt at peace with my decision. I told Bryan that he
needed to find a college in Florida because we would be
moving there after he graduates from high school.

I began upgrading the house, inside and outside, plus
the front and back yards. We took the above-ground pool
down, and a nice man came to take the pool deck apart
which I gave him, along with all the pool toys. I then
planted grass where the pool was located and flowers in a
rock garden. I built steps down to the basement level on
the side of the house out of railroad ties and stones. It was
very hard work rolling wheel barrels of stone from the
front yard around the side of the house, to the sloped back
yard, especially in the summer heat. I hired two men to

finish a few projects inside the house which were yet to be completed. Everything looked great both inside and outside.

My son, still had seven months of high school left before graduating. I did not want to sell the house too soon because we could not move until July, 2001, and it was only October, 2000. I decided to contact a realtor to see for how much the house could be sold. The realtor came in and loved the house. We had previously remodeled it less than two years ago. She listed it and said she did not think it would sell fast if we priced it high, so we had time. I told her I needed to stay in it seven more months. Well, she had people coming in and liking it very quickly. Long story made short the first person who came to see it, bought it. The house sold in three and a half weeks. The buyers wanted to close December 1, 2000, to be in their new home before Christmas. They offered full price, so I accepted it. There was one big problem - where would Bryan and I live for seven months? I searched all over our area for apartments to rent for seven months, with a dog. In New Jersey the rentals are for a year, not seven months. It was very difficult to find an apartment for a short - time, however, I did find a new mobile home park, more like modular homes, though, near our home. I had to stay in the same area so Bryan could finish his senior year in the same high school. My son did not like the idea of moving into a mobile home, coming from a house; that was the one and only place I could find. It really was nice in a new park and all modern inside. I liked that it was brand new, and no one had lived in it before. I explained to my son that this was all that was available. We moved in, and it worked out fine for the short term.

I immediately began looking on line for apartments in the Clearwater, Florida area. A friend of mine and her husband, who lived in the Tampa Bay area, went to take a look at the apartments that I had liked online. I had decided upon a new apartment complex with all the amenities, pools, hot tubs, car wash area, a running track, a clubhouse and in a gated community. Sounded great! I reserved the two-bedroom apartment, two baths. On July 1, 2001 we would be leaving New Jersey and moving to Florida, arriving on July 2nd.

The end of June, 2001, my son graduated from high school. I held a big graduation picnic for his friends and family at the park near our home. He was happy to be out of high school, and ready to move to Florida in a few weeks. I was getting excited to move - too, a new start for both of us.

My last Sunday at church, I walked up to the podium to say goodbye to my church family. I announced to the congregation I was moving to Clearwater, Florida. I said; "I do not know what I am to do there, but I feel in my heart that is where God is leading me." I also said, "I am going to try to sing a solo, if I can get through it without crying," I did have a few sniffles, but continued to sing the solo. After the solo, I thanked my church family for their love and support before leaving the podium. When the service ended people came up to me with tears in their eyes. They were sad to see me leave, but happy for me to

start a new chapter in my life. It was a bittersweet time for
me, as well. Once again, I said my goodbyes to everyone
in the lobby and received many hugs and kind words. I
exited the church feeling God's peace in my heart and
knowing it was time for me to be moving on.

What's Next

Moving day was finally here. We said our goodbyes to our friends and family. My brothers friend drove the moving truck with me and my dog, while my son drove his car with a friend. We arrived on July 2nd late in the afternoon. I could not get the apartment keys until July 3rd, so we spent a night in the hotel. The apartment complex was not too far from where the hotel was. In the morning we arrived at the apartments, and I went into the office to sign the lease. After I signed the lease, we drove to the apartment that I had rented. It was in a really nice, quiet location in the back of the complex. There was only one other family living in the entire building. Since it was a new complex, many people had not moved in yet. The guys unloaded the moving truck and I was in the apartment directing where things should go. At one point, I was becoming a little edgy. I went into my bedroom and prayed. After spending time with the Lord, I felt so much better.

My son and his friend decided to go for a ride to see the neighborhood. I began unpacking and playing with my dog, Toby. He had been in the moving truck driving to Florida for two days. Toby was only two years old and needed time to run around and play. I took him outside for a long walk, which he enjoyed, and so did I. Returning back to my apartment I began to unpack the boxes. The apartment was beginning to feel like home to me, and it was a good feeling.

On the 4th of July in the evening, I went with my friend and her husband to a restaurant on the water in a small town. I really enjoyed sitting outside on the patio and looking at the beautiful water and sunset. We later watched the fireworks from a dock, and the evening was perfect. God's peace was upon me. I was so happy the Lord brought me here; right now, this is where I wanted to be.

My days were filled with decorating the apartment, going to stores for household items, shopping for new furniture, etc. I spent a lot of time taking Toby out for walks around the complex and the big outdoor track area. The pools, and hot tub were plusses.

In August my son went off to college to live on campus. The day he left, I felt so sad. I knew he was going to leave me, and he would be only two hours away, but it seemed so much farther than it was. He packed his things, gave me a big hug, said goodbye and left the apartment. I missed him already, and had tears in my eyes. For a moment the memories came back to me when his father left in August two years ago. I said to myself that Bryan would be okay at school, and he will be back to visit his mom.

I was in search of a good church in the area. For me, going to church was an important part of my life. I liked being involved in a church and enjoyed singing in the choir. My girlfriend and I went to a local church in town and we did like it, but it was the same kind of church I came from in New Jersey. I told the Lord before I moved from New Jersey that when I move to Florida, I want to go to a different kind of church. I attended my church in New Jersey for ten years and enjoyed it, but I needed to learn more about God and wanted a closer spiritual walk. I was missing something!

I asked my girlfriend whose, name is also Cindy, if there were any Christian concerts in the area where we could go; I had never gone to one before. She looked around and found a Christian concert at a church called Countryside Christian Center (now Church) that was close to where I lived. We went to the concert on a Friday night and loved it. At the concert people were praising the Lord, lifting up their hands and had big smiles on their faces, singing songs with passion in their hearts. I had never seen this before. I liked the church a lot. On a Monday morning, I went to the main office of the church, and explained I was there on Friday night for a concert and really loved the music, praising Jesus. I wanted to know more about the church, and what their beliefs were. The receptionist handed me a piece of paper which was their Statement of Faith. I read

it all and yes, they believed what I believed: God the
Father, God the Son and God the Holy Spirit; Jesus is
Lord of all! I sat there for a few minutes talking with the
receptionist, and then a pastor came out to talk with me.
We somehow got into a conversation about learning more
about God. She went on to say we have a Training Center
(like a Bible school) offering all kinds of classes to help you
learn more about God. She said they were all accredited
classes. I told her I would like to attend some of these
classes. She sent me over to the administration office and
I spoke with the woman about which courses they offered.
Before I knew it, I had signed up full-time for nine
courses. I thought I only went to this church to attend a
Christian concert. This all happened so fast, visiting the
church office to see if they believed what I did, and the
next thing I know I am signed up for full-time school at
the Training Center. When, I told the Lord I wanted to go
to a different kind of church in Florida, this was the
church!

The pastor spoke about being baptized, immersed in
water as Jesus was, and I thought, I was only baptized as a
baby, a sprinkling - not immersed. At that moment, I
decided I wanted to be baptized in this church. I
contacted the office and made arrangements to do that. In
a couple of weeks our pastor would baptize people at a
Wednesday night service. I never knew we needed to be
fully immersed in the water. The night came and I was
ready to be baptized. My girlfriend, Cindy, also got
baptized that same night, as she had given her heart to
Jesus at the concert a month earlier. It was a wonderful

feeling. I rededicated my life to Jesus. People were clapping that we were baptized and were being obedient to God. Baptism does not get one to heaven, only Jesus does, but it is an obedience unto the Lord. After the service we went to the coffee shop for a snack to celebrate.

The Training Center classes began in September, and I was ready to learn. This was a whole new experience for me. I attended the Training Center every week day for the entire school year, from September until May. Nothing was going to stop me from learning and growing closer to God. There were tests, books to read, along with papers to write. One day I decided, I am taking too many classes and becoming overwhelmed. I needed to drop some of these courses so I could do my best. The next day, I went into the administrator's office and reduced my curriculum down to five courses. It was easier for me to maintain the reading of books, writing papers and tests with five courses instead of the nine courses. Before I knew it, that semester was over. I learned so much about the Lord from those courses and felt closer to Him. The Training Center was a wonderful experience for me.

God's Amazing Plans

The church presented many opportunities to volunteer.
One area where they needed volunteers was decorating the
banquet hall for events. I really enjoy decorating and
would sign up to help out. They usually had several men
and woman there helping. I met with two sweet ladies
who were in charge of the set up. Sometimes there were
only the two ladies, a man named Steve, and me to set up.
This began to happen more often than not; I was not sure
where all the other volunteers went. Steve and I worked
well together. One of the sweet ladies said jokingly "if you
two don't get together, I am going to put you together".
She was talking about Steve and me. We just laughed,
finished setting up and went our separate ways.

The church had a mid-week service on Wednesday
nights that my girlfriend and I attended every week.
Afterward, we would stop at a local coffee shop for
something to eat. Steve also attended the Wednesday

night services, and we would invite him to come along with us; he would meet us there. Sometimes, my girlfriend could not attend the church service on Wednesday night, so afterward Steve and I would stop at the coffee shop.

Steve first met me in the prayer room, however, we did not talk that much. The other times we would see each other was when we volunteered to set up the banquet hall for events, and on Sundays, since we were both in the choir.

I decided to get a part-time job at a Christian book store. Steve would stop in and bring me white chocolate mocha latte; as he knew that was my favorite. I would thank him and put it behind the counter. He seemed to linger in the store after handing me the coffee for quite some time. He said he was reading books. Hmmm…

A Christian concert in a nearby town was coming and I wanted to attend, but was not sure how to get there, and did not want to go by myself. I asked Steve if he wanted to join me, and, of course, he said yes. He offered to drive and said he could pick me up. I said thanks that would be okay. We had a good time at the concert and he dropped me off at my apartment and went on his way.

The next day I talked to my son on the phone and told him I went to a concert at the park with Steve. My son said to me, "Mom, you are so naïve - he likes you." I told him we were just friends. He laughed.

As time went on, we spent a lot of time together at the coffee shop just talking. I always paid for my own food and coffee even though Steve offered to pay for mine, because in my mind that would mean we were dating. I explained to Steve that my husband died a little over two years ago. He said he was sorry and I could tell he felt bad for me. I told him my faith is in God and He is always with me. He said, yes, He is always with us. Before leaving the parking lot, Steve asked me if he could pray for me; I said yes. He said a nice prayer, and we said goodnight and departed our own ways.

As I was driving home, I began to think Steve was a nice Christian man. He seemed to like me a little more than I liked him. I then realized I had never been with anyone else but Roy since I was sixteen years old. Something was beginning to develop, more than just friendship, on his end. I was not looking for a relationship with anyone, just friendship.

I was driving to the church one day by myself, and I heard God speak to me audibly, saying, "You are going to get married again someday." It was very clear; but I was not looking to get married again. I just kept driving and heard the same words a second time. I had told my church family in New Jersey that I was not going to Florida to get married. The ladies teased me and said, "Yes, you will". I kept saying "No, I am not."

On one occasion, I invited Steve over to my apartment for coffee in the evening instead of meeting at the coffee shop. I felt it would be okay. He came in and sat down on the sofa. I was sitting across the room from him on a chair. We talked for a bit, and then he handed me a card.

He went to sit back down on the sofa and I opened the card. It said, "I think I am beginning to fall in love with you." I probably had a look of surprise on my face. I thought we were just friends. Apparently, there was more to the story than I knew. He then came over to me, knelt down, took my hand and asked me to marry him. I felt like God was saying it's okay. I said, "Yes," and was at peace. Something happened after I said yes. It was as though God put a love in my heart (not just a friendship kind of love, a deep love) for Steve that I had not felt before. It happened so fast I could not even explain it. Steve told me that he did not have any intentions of coming over that evening talking about marriage. He said the Holy Spirit told him to come over to where I was sitting and asked me to marry him. Wow!!

"For My thoughts are not your thoughts, neither your ways My ways,' declares the Lord." Isaiah 55:8

We were married in nine months from when I heard the Lord speak to me. Our wedding ceremony was in the church sanctuary and a reception was upstairs in the banquet hall. Everyone had a great time, and they were so happy for us. God is in the center of our marriage, and Jesus is first in each of our lives. He has blessed us in so many ways, because of our obedience to Him.

Looking over all the things that happened since I began attending Countryside Christian Church, I am in awe of God's amazing plans, and what He has done in His timing and in His ways. He planned for me to meet my new husband, Steve, along with attending the Training Center to grow closer to Him, being baptized, and for almost five years I was employed by the church as the Decorating and Event Coordinator. I have been ordained as a pastor, not in the church, but through the church. I am so thankful to the Lord for redirecting me from a local church I was attending, to Countryside Christian Church.

When I felt the Lord was leading me to Clearwater, Florida, to a place I had never been before, and did not even know where it was, my complete trust was in Him. In my mind I could see a giant magnet pulling me there. I did what He told me to do.

"For I know the plans I have for you" declares the Lord," plans to prosper you and not to harm you, plans to give you hope and a future." Jeremiah 29:11

Get Up and Keep Going

We all go through storms in our life that is reality. Do we run from them or face them head on? No storm in our lives is bigger than our God. He will calm the waves which are crashing over you.

When my husband died suddenly, shock rocked my world and grief overcame me, but only for a time. I could not change what happened; I had to face what happened. There was only one way to do this, and that was with the Lord. God showed me if I gave all my pain to Him, He would take it from me. This burden was too big for me to handle on my own. I gave it all the Lord. I spent more time with Him in prayer and less time being wrapped up in my emotions. He carried me through the raging seas. I am weak, but He is strong.

Being on the mountain tops is a good place to be, but it's in the valleys we learn to depend on the Lord and begin to grow closer to Him. There are two things that happen when a loved one dies: either we draw closer to God or get further away from God. There is no in-between. For me, I drew closer to God and wanted more of Him and less of me. I loved talking to Him on my many walks. There is no peace like the peace of being in the presence of the Lord.

Get up! Look beyond your pain. Do not allow the disruptions in your life hold you back from the things God has for you - your purpose. Live it out for His glory. Stand firm in the Lord, stand on the rock, JESUS, and He will take you places you can't even imagine. As Christians we have hope, our hope is in the Lord. The world does not offer any hope. I went through grief with hope that God was going to restore me.

"But I will hope continually, and will praise you yet more and more." Psalm 71:14

"But those who hope is in the Lord will renew their strength. They will soar on wings like eagles; they will run and not grow weary; they will walk and not faint." Isaiah 40:31

Walk Out Your Purpose

After everything I had experienced, I could have been mad at God, or become a bitter person - none of which happened. I love the Lord and wanted Him to use me for His purposes. It's not about me; it is all about God. He knew my heart was His.

One day the Lord spoke to me about becoming a Christian counselor. I wanted to make sure I heard Him correctly because I was fifty-seven years old, and the thought of going back to school at that age was going to be both challenging and exciting. I said "Yes Lord." I began looking for an accredited Christian Counseling school. After researching on line I found a school that specializes in this field. I applied, and after taking a 500-question biblical test, along with 50 Board of Examiners questions I was approved and accepted. In 2012 I received my Bachelor of Arts degree. I continued working toward my

Master's degree which I received in 2014 at the age of sixty. Age does not matter to God, obedience does. The Holy Spirit helped me through school by giving me the insight, wisdom, and the fortitude to keep going. As a Licensed Christian Counselor, the Lord has entrusted me to do His work here on the earth to help His people.

He has a purpose and a plan for each of us to fulfill. I encourage you, do not get stuck in grief. Make up your mind, "I will not get stuck in grief." We all need to go through the grieving process at our own pace. The only way to get through it is to go through it. To go through something means to pass by it, not dwell in it.

When going through the grieving process, it's best to look for an opportunity to help someone, whether it is a friend, relative or even a stranger. In doing so, you will be a blessing to others, and at the same time they will be a blessing to you.

During the time I was grieving, my pastor who was recently transferred from another church was new to the area needed help updating the parsonage. I volunteered to wallpaper her dining room. She was so appreciative that I wanted to bless her. Her kitchen needed painting; so, she painted while I wallpapered. At that time, we both needed a friend, and my purpose was to help her.

Every day we wake up, we have a purpose. Look for it. Ask the Lord to show you your purpose daily.

In my story, Roy died, but Cindy went on living, fulfilling her purpose for God's Glory!

Author's Page

Cindy Rogers is a Licensed Clinical Pastoral Counselor and a Certified Temperament Counselor, along with being an ordained pastor, not at - but through, my local church.

I have a practice - Living Well Christian Counseling located in Florida since 2012.

I am a member of the National Christian Counseling Association.

I graduated with a Bachelor of Arts degree in Christian Counseling, 2012, and a Master of Clinical Christian Counseling degree 2014. My areas of counseling are in marriage, family, pre-marital and grief, with grief counseling being my primary. In addition to counseling one on one, I also facilitate a Christian Grief program in a group setting.

Along with counseling, I teach Bible studies at various locations such as: YMCA, church, rehab center, retirement communities, at the park and in people's homes.

As a grief counselor, I can personally relate to others going through grief since I have experienced it firsthand with the tragic death of my husband. I truly understand how my clients feel and comfort them with the same comfort God gave me when I was grieving.

One morning upon awakening, I felt the Lord speak to me about writing a book on my grief experience. I told

Him, "I do not know how to write a book," and that I needed His help. He wanted me to share my story with others who are overwhelmed with grief to let them know that He is with them and will always be with them, forever. In your deepest saddest moments seek God, sense His presence and feel His love for you.

When I sat down to write this book, on grief, both the chapter titles and the story flowed. I know, the Holy Spirit was bringing back to my remembrance the way things happened during my horrific tragedy, and was helping me to write expressively, so others could understand the message. I am not a writer; I express myself verbally, and that is why my calling is in counseling. I have the gift of talking - not writing. Only by the grace of God could I have written this book, and He gets all the glory!

I am sharing my story with others how the Lord can take not just a broken heart, but a shattered heart that feels like it's been crushed, and bring it back to a living heart, a vibrant heart, and once again, a loving heart.

Salvation

You can know for sure where you will spend eternity.

In John 14:6 Jesus answered, *"I am the way and the truth and the life. No one comes to the Father except through me."*

Jesus Christ went to the cross willingly and died for all mankind for the forgiveness of our sins.

Romans 5:8 *"But God demonstrates His own love toward us, in that while we were still sinners, Christ died for us."*

My passion is for everyone to receive Jesus Christ into their hearts as his or her Lord and Savior.

How do I receive Jesus Christ into my heart and make Him my Lord and Savior?

Repent of your sins.

Ask Jesus to forgive you.

Ask Jesus to come into your heart and be your Lord and Savior.

Salvation Prayer

Dear Jesus, I know I am a sinner and I am truly sorry for the sins I have committed. I repent of my sins, and I ask you to forgive me. I believe you died in my place on the cross for the forgiveness of my sins, and on the third day, God raised you from the dead. I ask you, Lord Jesus, to come into my heart and be my Lord and Savior. I thank you for saving me. In Jesus name. Amen.

"For it is by grace you have been saved, through faith — and this is not from yourselves, it is the gift of God — not by works, so that no one can boast." Ephesians 2:8-9

How do I grow closer to the Lord?

Find a good Bible-teaching church. Read the Bible daily, along with spending time in prayer. Jesus speaks to us through His Word (the Bible) and during our times with Him in prayer. The way to build a relationship with the Lord is spending time with Him.

Jesus wants a relationship with us - not religion.

www.ingramcontent.com/pod-product-compliance
Lightning Source LLC
Chambersburg PA
CBHW030403160726
47992CB00007B/2947